The Universal Catechism

A HOMILY SOURCEBOOK

D1601528

The Universal Catechism

A HOMILY SOURCEBOOK

N. Abeyasingha

The Pastoral Press
Washington, DC

ISBN: 1-56929-010-5

The Pastoral Press
225 Sheridan Street, N.W.
Washington, D.C. 20011
(202) 723-1254

The Pastoral Press is the publications division of the National Association
of Pastoral Musicians, a membership organization of musicians and clergy
dedicated to fostering the art of musical liturgy.

Printed in the United States of America

Contents

Introduction

Somewhere at the intersection of the biblical memory of redemption, the liturgical celebration of that redemption made actual and present today, and expected norms of behavior lies what can be called "The Way" (see Acts 9:2)—the Christian form of life, the "culture" in which the followers of Jesus live and interact, the culture that transmits this heritage from generation to generation.

The Christian form of life is first of all a human way of life; and then, it is a call to re-create our humanity after the model of THE HUMAN ONE, namely, Jesus the Christ in whom, the believer claims, is the full and definitive revelation of God. But because the Christian way of life is first a human form of life, progress in human sciences has impacted on the communication of the Christian heritage. The biblical narrative certainly enshrines the memory of whatever heritage can claim to call itself Christian. This narrative drew from the modes of communication of that time. Today we need to communicate this same memory in a manner appropriate to our times.

Today we are still at the intersection, an intersection which has become a major crossroads. So many human sciences have also met at this point. It has become almost impossible to use a word without someone crying "foul." Say that God is "Father" and someone will ask "Why not Mother?" Say that God saves us from sin, and very quickly there will be a discussion whether the emphasis should be on

1

personal sin or structural sin. Say that the resurrection is an historical event, and someone will pose the problem that only the empirically verifiable and repeatable can be considered historical. We can go on and on.

We need to be honest and admit that we need, as always, to *communicate* the Christian message. The biblical categories have always needed to be supplemented and complemented in various ways by other terms and categories so that communication can take place. This has been true throughout history. With the *aggiornamento* ("bringing up to date") that was effected by Vatican II, many aspects of the Christian form of life were re-examined and re-stated in such a manner that they could be communicated to and understood by contemporary society.

Updating, however, is not the overturning of Tradition. Practically 80 percent of traditional knowledge is stable, hardly changing over decades, even centuries. But there is also about 20 percent of our knowledge that does change. Should we cry "foul" to anything that is communicated on the basis of the 20 percent? Do we really need in our communication to highlight the 20 percent that is fashionable and downplay the 80 percent that is stable? We communicate on the basis of what is stable. This is our common heritage. This is where our identity is rooted.

Communication is always inadequate, especially when communicating God's revelation in Jesus. In attempting to communicate this revelation, we try to communicate what is ultimately a mystery—the gratuitous communication of a free God to a people whose imagination is sinful from its youth (see Gen 8:21). We are not speaking of God as an object like a chair or a table. God has first "broken into" our lives. Concepts about God and discussions about the nature of that action have followed in our attempt to communicate that event and that experience. Proclamation is continuing communication. But communication needs an idiom and a grammar. And this idiom and the grammar need to be "common" because they belong to a "public world"; for the Christian, the idiom and grammar belong to the Christian community. No one is free to give this idiom and grammar of communication "private" meaning. But do we have a common idiom and a common grammar of communication today?

The ministry of proclaiming God's word, especially in the Sunday liturgy, has often fatigued ministers and brought them close to despair. On the one hand, as they read the Scripture assigned for the Sunday, they catch a "glimpse" of the truth. On the other hand, they are enmeshed in the dominant value systems and popular theories of the day. It is in this context that I write this little booklet. How can the glimpse of truth be communicated in the face of contemporary resistance to truth?

My contention is that Vatican II re-affirmed the Tradition. In doing so it provided us with a *common idiom and a common grammar* The *Catechism of the Catholic Church*, recently published in various vernacular editions, attempts to present this common idiom and grammar. Why not re-learn and re-affirm the idiom and grammar of the Tradition (as it is reflected in the Catechism) and re-read and— especially in our liturgy—re-proclaim this Tradition as an invitation to faith and repentance (by referring ourselves to the salvific memory enshrined in the Scripture readings of each Sunday)? Perhaps in this way we will begin to communicate. Perhaps we may regain vitality in our ministry by refusing to protect ourselves and others from the truth of the Gospel. Perhaps in the liturgy we, like the great prophets, will not be afraid to realize that God is a God who acts; that God's action is certain even though it is unpredictable.

The proposal presented in the following pages is simply this:

• We need a common idiom and a common grammar; other-wise, we cannot communicate. This common idiom gives us an extensive knowledge of specifics that are a vital part of "The Way," namely, the culture that we can call Christian.

• Each Sunday we meet as a celebrating community and hear the word of God proclaimed, calling us to faith and conversion. This celebration provides us with a rather intensive experience of rela-tionships within the Christian community.

• Why not use the occasion and opportunity of the celebration to hear the homiletic proclamation in a common idiom and using a common grammar? In this way we grow to be a people joined together by a common culture; we become a communion because we communicate in the word, in the Mystery, in a "Communion of Saints." What we do in the liturgical celebration and in our life will give sense to what we say.

10 January 1993   N. Abeyasingha.

Homiletics, Catechesis, and the Catechism

The renewal of the church's worship as envisioned by Vatican II emphasized the liturgy as reactualizing the Paschal Mystery. This emphasis can be found in the post-conciliar reform of the sacramental rites. Even though the renewal of the church through the renewal of its liturgy has not been accomplished to the extent hoped for at the time of the council, still the church has been renewed through its renewed liturgy, and many aspects of this renewed liturgy will remain long into the future. One such feature is the primacy accorded both to the proclamation of God's word in the liturgy and to the homily which explains this word (see the Constitution on the Sacred Liturgy, no. 24). In the light of the publication of the New or Universal Catechism (it's officially called the *Catechism of the Catholic Church*), the question is whether the Sunday homily can serve as a means for catechesis.

The Catechetical Content of the Homily

The parish community is called to gather each Sunday for the eucharist. It can be argued that Sunday worship is the only time most people have, not just to read, but to listen to God's word and hear its call for renewal. Our first task is to understand the nature of this people, the nature of the assembly that gathers together for the liturgy.

The liturgical assembly is composed of people who share a common faith, a people who gather in response to the call of God's word. Christ is present among this people (see Constitution on the Sacred Liturgy, no. 7) who gather not merely to *listen* and respond to God's word, but also to *celebrate* God's word and to commit themselves to *live* out this word. The liturgical celebration builds up the community of believers so that its members might carry out their mission to the world. Through word and song, gesture and action, the liturgical celebration incarnates the faith of the assembly, expressing the mystery of the ever-present God revealed in Jesus Christ and shared in the Spirit. Thus the liturgical assembly is not primarily an educational assembly. It is not a classroom. It is a celebrating assembly.

To say that the liturgical assembly is not an "educational assembly" does not mean that educational aspects are totally excluded. Once the faithful have gathered together, they can and should be evangelized—can and should be called to faith and repentance (see Constitution on the Sacred Liturgy, no. 9). They can and should respond to the *kerygma*. This is clearly expressed by Pope Paul VI in his *Evangelii Nuntiandi* (referred to in nos. 1074-1075 of the New Catechism). Pope Paul VI says:

> In these times when the liturgy renewed by the Council has given greatly increased value to the liturgy of the word, it would be a mistake not to see in the homily an important and very adaptable instrument of evangelization. Of course it is necessary to know and put to good use the requirements and the strengths of the homily, so that it will reach its full pastoral effectiveness. But above all it is particularly necessary for each individual to be convinced of this effectiveness and to bring to it the dedication of a total love. When integrated in a special way into the eucharistic action from which it receives its proper force and vigor, this kind of preaching certainly has a particular role in evangelization, because it expresses the sacred minister's profound faith and is suffused with love (*Evangelii Nuntiandi*, no. 43).

Catechesis is evangelization, but in a different key. By means of catechesis we learn "through systematic religious instruction the fundamental teachings, the living content of the truth which God has wished to convey to us and which the Church has sought to express in an ever richer fashion during the course of her long history" (*Evangelii Nuntiandi*, no. 43). The liturgy is not the place for this. Catechesis within the liturgical homily is not systematic religious instruction. Pope Paul VI says:

> The faithful assembled as a Paschal Church, celebrating the feast of the Lord present in their midst [the liturgical assembly] expect much from this preaching [the liturgical homily], and will greatly benefit from it [the call to faith and repentance issuing in a commitment to their mission to the world] provided that it is simple, clear, direct, well-adapted, profoundly dependent on Gospel teaching and faithful to the Magisterium, animated by a balanced apostolic ardor coming from its own characteristic nature, full of hope, fostering belief and productive of peace and unity. Many parochial or other communities live and are held together thanks to the Sunday homily, when it possesses these qualities (*Evangelii Nuntiandi*, no. 43; insertions mine).

The liturgical homily is an *opportunity* for catechesis. However, the homily is not primarily and directly catechetical. Catechesis, namely, the systematic handing-on of the church's doctrinal heritage, is a point of reference for the liturgical homily.

The Liturgical Homily

The liturgical homily should have pride of place (see *Dei Verbum*, no. 23). "By means of the homily, the mysteries of the faith and the guiding principles of the Christian life are expounded from the sacred text during the course of the liturgical year" (Constitution on the Sacred Liturgy, no. 52). "Its character should be a proclamation of God's wonderful works in the history of salvation, that is the mystery of Christ made present and active within us especially in the celebration of the liturgy" (Constitution on the Sacred Liturgy, no. 35:1).

The approach of the Catechism is basically an endorsement of these same perspectives. The Catechism itself speaks of the *liturgy of the word* as being an integrating part of sacramental celebrations. To nourish the faith of the faithful, the signs of the God's word should be given prominence: the book of the word (lectionary or evangeliary), its veneration (procession, incense, light), the place of the word's announcement (the ambo), its audible and intelligible reading, the homily which prolongs the proclamation of the word, the assembly's responses, namely, acclamations, psalms of meditation, litanies, confession of faith (see nos. 1154, 1100-1102).

Kerygma, Didache, and the Homily

The liturgical homily is an *opportunity* for catechesis. But it is a catechesis that takes place within the movement and dynamic of the liturgy. In revelation God reveals himself: "*I* am the Lord." Both the evangelizer and the catechist proclaim this word. Both say "Jesus is Lord." However, the audience to whom the proclamation is addressed are different; the goals which each seeks to realize are different. The evangelizer makes his or her proclamation to those who are not yet Christians hoping that their hearts may be opened by the Holy Spirit and that they may believe and be freely converted to the Lord. The catechist makes his or her announcements to those who already believe in order that they may better understand the Lord whom they profess and seek to follow. The response which the evangelizer seeks to evoke is "Yes, *he* is Lord." This response changes the non-believer into a believer. The response which the catechist strives for is: "Yes *he* is Lord; within the Tradition of those who believe; he is *consubstantial* with the Father [Council of Nicea], *true God, true man* [Council of Chalcedon], etc." The catechist expects to draw this response from the believer. Through catechesis the believer is led to a deeper understanding of the Tradition and comes to a clearer conceptual grasp of the faith, which he or she already professes. In the liturgy the person who has accepted the message of the evangelizer (and responded in faith sealed by the sacrament of faith) and the Tradition mediated to him or her by the catechist (to the extent of his or her capacity) *together* with the community of believers proclaims: "*You* are Lord" with praise and thanksgiving. The liturgical profession of faith is the context within which the liturgical homily is preached. It is a movement from faith to knowledge to praise and worship. The homily can focus particularly on one or other of these elements, but it should not exclude any of the other elements. In this sense liturgical catechesis is a qualified catechesis.

When a liturgical homily is preached, there is a teacher-taught relationship. But it is not one in which the teacher knows everything there is to be known and the taught has only to learn. It is a process of growing in commitment and deeper engagement in following Jesus. The Rite for the Christian Initiation of Adults (no. 4) expresses this well. "The initiation of catechumens takes place step by step in the midst of the community of the faithful. Together with the catechumens, the faithful reflect upon the value of the paschal mystery, renew their own conversion, and by their example lead the catechumens to obey the Holy Spirit more generously." What is said of Christian Initiation holds for the entire range of liturgical action.

Because of the renewal of conversion that is called for by the very nature of the Christian life and especially when the Christian community meets to celebrate its constitutive memory in the liturgy, believers have to refer themselves back to the basic elements of the Gospel (*kerygma*). But because their celebration takes place in a world that is no longer the world of the New Testament, they need to accept those elements that have entered into the Tradition to explain the faith and to provide answers for new questions. This is the doctrinal heritage of the church (*didache*), which does not confine itself to scriptural terminology.

The non-scriptural term "consubstantial" did not exist as part of the Tradition prior to the Council of Nicea. But since that time the term forms part of the Tradition. The term was used to answer a question that was not raised in the scriptural tradition. This term found a place in the creed (profession of faith). It kept the community of believers united (*koinonia*). New questions have been raised over the centuries; answers have been formulated to which all believers can say "Amen." This further elaboration and systematic exposé of faith contributes to a better understanding of faith.

The Christian life of those who believed and have been incorporated into the church through baptism constantly refers itself back to the *kerygma* to renew its conversion; it seeks to understand the faith by a better understanding of the Tradition (*didache*); it seeks to grow into a fellowship (*koinonia*) and to engage in right living and good works (*orthopraxis*) and are united in praise and worship (*orthodoxa*). All this activity has its ultimate point of reference in the word that is proclaimed. And it is this word that is celebrated in the liturgy. Which of these elements the liturgical homily should highlight will depend on the nature of the assembly. But whichever element the homily highlights, its overall role is to integrate the word proclaimed, the word lived in life, and the word celebrated in the sacramental action.

Acts 2:42 says that the baptized "devoted themselves to the apostles' teaching (*didache*) and fellowship, to the breaking of bread and the prayers." In what is evidently a liturgical celebration at Troas (Acts 20:7-12), Paul conversed with the members of the community (*dielegeto*), prolonged his sermon (*logos*), and gave them a discourse (*homilesas*). Evidently, all this took place within the liturgical action. Thus, more took place than the proclamation of the Gospel. These further elaborations of the primary proclamation have a proper place in the liturgy. We need to try to understand what this place is.

The Prologue of the Catechism says that the goal of this book is to present an organic and synthetic exposé of the essential and fundamental content of Catholic doctrine on both faith and morals, doing so in the light of the Second Vatican Council and of the ensemble of the church's Tradition. The principal sources of the Catechism are Holy Scripture, the holy Fathers, the liturgy, and the magisterium of the church. We are told that the book is intended to be a point of reference for catechisms or compendia which are composed in various countries. As to the readers of the book, the Prologue says that the Catechism is meant principally for those responsible for catechesis: in the first place for bishops since they are teachers of the faith and pastors of the church. It is offered as an instrument in the fulfillment of their responsibility of teaching the People of God. Through the bishops, this work is also directed to the redactors of catechisms, to priests, and to catechists. It will also be useful reading for all the Christian faithful as well.

The Catechism presents the Tradition of the Church. It represents the Tradition that has received the endorsement of Vatican II. In our day one can arguably assert that this Tradition has been taken for granted. Specific themes based on dominant concerns have been explicitly discussed and elaborated. It has been presumed that the "common sense" and "conventional wisdom" of the Christian Tradition are known as a common heritage. Our question is: Are the terms used to state the Tradition known in such a way that every believer who uses the terms does so in basically the same sense? Experience leads us to answer the question in the negative.

And hence, our proposal. When believers meet together to celebrate the liturgy, one of the elements that the homilist does well to emphasize and proclaim is the content of what we hold in common—our common Tradition as followers of Jesus expressed in a common idiom (a set of terms) and a common grammar (the terms put together in a very specific way) to which all believers say "Amen." It is for this purpose that the Catechism is a handy work of reference for homilists.

The Shape of the Homily

While emphasizing the Catechism as a source from which one can gather content for the homily, it is also important to remember that the *liturgical* homily represents a particular genre of preaching. Its characteristics have been formulated in the teaching of Pope Paul VI (see *Evangelii Nuntiandi*, no. 43). The homily is biblical, liturgical, and kerygmatic. Its style is that of familiar conversation.

The Homily as Biblical

Justin, describing a second-century liturgy, refers to the biblical nature of the homily: "when the reader has finished [the readings], the president of the assembly verbally admonishes and invites all to imitate such examples of virtue" (1 Apol 67). The homily is not an act of reporting on an old text. It is the act of making the old text (the passage that has been proclaimed) visible and available to *this* assembled community. This "new" text (the homily) is in part the old text, and is in part the imaginative construction of the preacher. This new aspect does not exist until it is uttered by the preacher.

The homilist interprets without argument. In doing so, one constructs something new. However, in constructing the "new" text, the preacher is objective. He or she is not a dreamer who believes that a private world can be conjured up and set before one's hearers. The preacher recognizes that this assembly builds on the heritage of many generations of followers of Christ. But this objectivity does not assume that the world is closed, fixed, and unchangeable. God's wonderful deeds can be renewed in this world. The homilist acknowledges his or her own need of redemption. So, the interpretation is from a "wounded" (sinful) interpreter and takes place in a world where several other elements, elements that are unredeemed, exert their influence. The constant reference to the salvific memory as enshrined in the biblical text is the in-built principle of renewal. It becomes a principle of renewal insofar as it is kerygmatic—a focus on the one proclaimed rather than on the one proclaiming.

The Homily as Kerygma

When we speak of the homily as kerygmatic we mean that it is a proclamation of the Good News. In this proclamation Jesus Christ is preached. It is not doctrine defended, but the wonderful deeds of God boldly announced. It does not impose or attempt to persuade. It repeats the call so succinctly expressed as the summary of Jesus' ministry, at the beginning of Mark's Gospel: "The time is fulfilled, and the kingdom of God is at hand; repent and believe in the Gospel" (Mk 1:15).

A model of such kerygmatic proclamation within the liturgical action would be the heart-to-heart discourse between the "stranger" (the unrecognized Jesus) and the disciples on the road to Emmaus. The discourse here is familiar. But it is a call to faith, a call bringing back in strong language the message of the Scripture. "O foolish men and slow of heart to believe (*pisteuein*) all that the prophets have spoken! Was it not necessary that Christ should suffer these things and so enter into his glory? And beginning with Moses and all the prophets, he interpreted (*diermeneusen* = explained without argument) in all the Scripture the things concerning himself" (Lk 24:25-27). The "stranger" did not force an invitation from the disciples, but when the disciples invited him to stay with them (a response to the conversation, which was also a proclamation), their eyes were opened (see Lk 24:28-32).

Whereas *kerygma* is primarily proclamation, the New Testament sometimes joins proclamation to "teaching" (see Mt 4:23, 9:35, 11:1; Acts 28:31). A lively debate took place during the Second Vatican Council as to whether the liturgical homily should be kerygmatic or catechetical. There was no clear decision. The Constitution on the Liturgy uses both the word "sermon" (no. 35) and "homily" (no. 52). The 1983 Code of Canon Law, following no. 52 of the Constitution, uses the word "homily" in its section on the Teaching Office of the Church (canon 767). Thus the emphasis is on the aspect of proclamation.

The word of God is *proclaimed* in the liturgy, and the homily continues that proclamation. Proclamation means that the acceptance of the content invites the assembly to faith and conversion. This faith-conversion is not primarily expressed in words that clarify the content of the faith, but rather in words of praise to God for God's gifts, and in petition/intercession for ourselves and for the whole world. It is also expressed in commitment within the body of believers and in service to the world. The Catechism in dealing with the eucharist cites, for example, John Chrysostom: "You have tasted the blood of the Lord and you do not recognize your brother. You dishonor this very table . . ." (no. 1397). What takes place in this liturgical interaction is an affirmation by doxology or praise. If argument is needed, then it is by polemic. "Our God is in the heavens; he does whatever he pleases. *Their* idols are silver and gold, the work of human hands. They have mouths, but do not speak; eyes, but do not see . . . " (Ps 115:3-4).

The Homily: Within the Liturgical Action

The basic movement of the liturgy is *from* the Father *through* the Son *in* the Spirit *to* the Father. For this movement to occur, there must be a response of faith from the assembly. This is why the proclamation of the Gospel focuses especially on the demands and pre-conditions for a response that accepts the Good News. Even the creed as professed in the liturgy is an act of praise and worship; it articulates the basis upon which we gather together. The Catechism rightly says that we do not believe in formulas, but in the realities which these formulas express and which faith permits us to "touch" (see no. 170). It is by touching the realities of faith in the liturgy that the assembly and the entire world is transformed.

Xavier Léon-Dufour in his book *Sharing the Eucharistic Bread* (pp. 72-76) offers a useful summary of the structure and meaning of the various relationships that are built around the account of the Lord's Supper. These relationships, structured around a single agent, Jesus, bring into the scene the totality of what is real: God, creation, people of all times. Jesus becomes the one who is absent-and-present. His "body" is no longer the body that others used to see. He now expresses himself through the bread and the cup and through the disciples whom the bread and cup unite to him. The covenant is concluded in Jesus. The *disciples* are transformed by being associated in the transformation that affects Jesus himself. By eating the one bread and drinking from the one cup, they become one body, living by one life, which is Jesus himself. In this way the *created world* finds its full meaning. The food received from God becomes a fraternal meal—a source of unity among those at table—and an expression of the covenant.

Who is the author of the change that affects Jesus, the disciples, and the created world itself? This change is not due to the gathering for a meal nor to the eating; it is caused by *the word of Jesus*. This word, which is a prophetic word, is not meant as a commentary on a new rite; rather, it effects the change by the very act of being spoken. According to biblical tradition, the word of God is not a simple announcement but an action. In the eucharist, this action takes concrete form in the gesture of distributing the bread and the cup.

If we go beyond an analysis of the structure of the scriptural narrative of the Lord's Supper, we can ask whether the word of Jesus proclaimed takes concrete form only in the distribution of the bread and cup? The obvious answer is that it does not. From the earliest times there have been other manifestations of the commitment to which the first proclamation (*kerygma*) calls us. The liturgical celebration has four dimensions: a memorial of the past; a celebration of a present actualization; a pledge of the future and a sign of commitment. In all these dimensions we are part of a long chain of witnesses who draw their strength and inspiration from the liturgical celebration.

The Homily: Familiar Conversation

It was Origen (185-253) who distinguished between *logos* or *sermo* (sermon) and *homilia* or *tractatus* (homily). Whereas the sermon followed the shape of classical rhetoric, the homily was direct and free. The sermon often relied on biblical texts to prove a doctrinal point, and yet it was *not rooted* in the biblical text. It was especially with Augustine that the sermon entered into popular usage. With his training in rhetoric, Augustine borrowed from the rhetorical canons to teach, to please, and to persuade. He deplored poorly fashioned homilies and encouraged preachers to learn from the persuasive rhetoric of his day (see his *De Doctrina Christiana* 4).

Vatican II offered no model for the specific nature of the homily. The Council merely said that the homily should be rooted in the biblical readings or the texts of the liturgy itself. We find more in the words of Pope Paul VI who said that the homily is to be "simple, clear, direct, well-adapted, profoundly dependent on gospel teaching . . ." (*Evangelii Nuntiandi*, no. 43). Thus, the homily belongs to the genre of familiar discourse, and in such discourse there is a mixture of communal activity, available information, imagination, myth, and even vested interests.

The homily is poetry of a particular type. John Heath- Stubbs in his poem "Ars Poetica" writes that

> . . . poetry is not "emotional truth."
> The emotions have much less to do with the business
> Than is commonly supposed. No more than the intellect.
> The intellect shapes, the emotions feed the poem,
> Whose roots are in the senses, whose flower is imagination.

The "intellect" that shapes the "poetic" elements that are integrated within the homily is the memory of salvation. This memory announces the present moment as a manifestation of God's mighty deeds through the word proclaimed and the liturgical action celebrated.

Incorporating Catechesis in the Homily

Can the proclamation of the Gospel in the liturgical homily be combined with catechesis? The short answer to the question is "Yes." But the "Yes" needs to be qualified in the light of what has already been said. Systematic teaching of the doctrinal heritage of the church must have a setting outside the liturgy. Knowledge that is transmitted within the liturgy presupposes faith and leads to praise and worship. One can offer a telling example of this approach. Even though we live several centuries after Copernicus, we still say "The sun rises," "The sun sets." This is scientifically inaccurate. But such knowledge is sufficient to regulate our normal rhythm of life. No one challenges its truth in ordinary discourse. Even the aircraft pilot uses such language in ordinary discourse. And yet he or she better not pilot the flight path of the aircraft on that basis. What the Catechism offers is the common heritage of knowledge to which all believers can answer "Amen." It is a basic knowledge, which is sufficient for all believers to regulate the ordinary course of their lives.

The Catechism gives what is or should be the common idiom and the common grammar affirmed by Vatican II. This common idiom and grammar can be used to communicate the call to faith today and to communicate the knowledge that is required to follow Jesus today. In the liturgy, the Gospel is always proclaimed as the marvelous works of God taking place today and inviting the community to hear and respond to that call today. Therefore, the link is in terms of *communication*. The Catechism provides the preacher with a common idiom in which to translate and communicate the Gospel proclaimed in the liturgy.

The New Catechism itself sees that proclamation and teaching are two clearly distinct areas, striving for two different goals. More importantly, the readership envisaged for the New Catechism is certainly smaller than the numbers of those who participate in the liturgy. The Catechism is primarily for teachers of the faith; it is proposed as useful reading for other Christian faithful. On the other hand, the liturgy is the very life of the church. The early martyrs cried out "We cannot live without the eucharist." The liturgy is the summit toward which the activity of the church is directed; it is the font from which all its power flows. Through the liturgy the work of our redemption is accomplished. Full and active participation in the liturgy is for *all* Christians without exception, not merely by way of exhortation, but as right, duty, and privilege. It sustains the hope that "as King, he [Jesus the Christ] claims dominion over all creation, that he may present to you, his almighty Father, an eternal and universal kingdom, a kingdom of truth and life, a kingdom of holiness and grace, a kingdom of justice, love and peace" (Preface, Feast of Christ the King).

Is full, conscious, and active participation possible without a common idiom? Without some form of words to which the entire assembly can say "Amen"? Without a common "grammar" which all who celebrate the liturgy can accept, namely, a grammar that uses words in certain contexts and rejects the use of these words in other contexts?

The Catechism recalls that the liturgy is the privileged place of catechesis. And catechesis is, in fact, intrinsically linked to the entire liturgical and sacramental action because it is in the sacraments, and especially in the eucharist, that Jesus Christ acts fully for the transformation of human persons. Liturgical catechesis, we are told, seeks to be an introduction into the mystery of Christ (it is "mystagogy"). It proceeds from the visible to the invisible, from the signifying to signified, from the "sacraments" to the "mysteries" (see nos. 1074-1075).

I suggest, then, that we can envisage the combination of catechesis with the liturgical homily from a very specific point of view—from what the Catechism calls "mystagogy." It is a catechesis that is integrated into the action of the liturgy and remains a proclamation and a call to a response of faith-conversion in life and action. This type of catechesis gives a *conceptual focus* to that call.

The conceptual focus is neither a language game nor a matter of playing around with abstractions. The conceptual focus means that we use words that carry a meaning shared by all believers. It is not accepting a system. It is description and explanation. The word that is used "evokes" the same "information" in all who share the common culture or sub-culture that we call "Christian." We are informed in order to offer praise and thanksgiving for God's wonderful works wrought in our midst today. Anything less is to generate followers of Jesus who are over-catechized and under-evangelized, followers who know the faith and can argue about it but who can hardly worship the God who overturns "idols" and who claims our absolute loyalty.

To absolutize the present, to limit our imagination to reason is the fruit of the Enlightenment. As children of the Enlightenment, we subscribe to modes of power that pretend autonomy; modes of reason that control; modes of economy that monopolize. But is this the totality of the enormous gift of human reason, human freedom, and human possibility? Today we realize, more than ever, that it is not so.

The basis of hope is the memory that is enshrined in the Gospel as proclaimed, especially in the liturgy. Biblical memory leads to praise. Why praise? Because praise enables us to disengage ourselves from the dominant reality. Because biblical faith enables us to see that dominant cultural perspectives deny grief, co-opt holiness, and nullify memory in the interest of an absolute present. The present is not absolute; we are pilgrims journeying toward the final age.

The Gospel has to be proclaimed in today's world, a world which is quite different from that of biblical times. We need a language that people today can understand; yet not any language whatsoever; not words that are given arbitrary meaning. It is here that the Catechism gives the post-Vatican II church a common idiom and a common grammar. Catechesis using the Catechism can recall in language that we can understand today what we remember, what we celebrate, what we can hope for, and how we can concretely express our commitment.

What Kind of Catechesis?

The specific nature of the liturgical homily imposes certain limitations as to the kind of catechesis that can be imparted through it. Some Sunday gospels, for example, are not cited in the Catechism. Neither can the Catechism be considered a compendium of the church's magisterium. There are only selected references from the ecumenical councils. Pope Leo XIII's *Rerum Novarum* is not cited, even though the church's social doctrine is incorporated into the book. Therefore the Catechism needs to be considered as a witness to the post-Vatican II faith of the People of God verified through the resident bishops. It is a monument in words that belongs to our times.

On the other hand, the liturgy permits us to "touch" the realities which catechesis expounds. As such, the liturgical action basically calls for a response of faith and conversion expressed in commitment. This call is non-thematic. There is little speculation about issues. The demand repeated in a variety of ways is "Make sure you are on the right path" (see Lk 13:23-24). It is a call that transcends our moment of history. The response of faith and conversion called for carries us forward to the "Last Times." Therefore there should be no attempt to insert into a celebratory action of this nature a thematic, conceptual, discursive presentation of faith.

This is not to say that catechesis is unimportant. And yet only a particular type of catechesis has a place within the liturgical homily. Certainly there are many things that are good to know. Technical distinctions, scholarly discussions about the history of doctrine, and the like have a place in theology, but not in liturgical catechesis. What is celebrated in the liturgy is what *all* believers are called to understand, and by understanding to enter into the mystery itself, to be "divinized."

A Suggestion on How to Incorporate Catechesis in Liturgical Preaching

Today we are speaking a Babel of "private" languages. We use the same words, and yet we mean quite different things. As a result we do not communicate, we cannot communicate. The Catechism provides us with a certain form of words used in very particular contexts. Here we have words that are assigned a very specific content. Let us use them to *communicate* the Gospel—let us use them as the *common idiom and the common grammar of the post-Vatican II universal church.*

In every society much is taken for granted in the interactions occurring within that society. Unless we are acquainted with what is taken for granted, we remain "outsiders" to that society. These matters fall into two broad areas. First, we need a certain degree of knowledge. This knowledge need not be complete, but it must focus upon specifics. Second, we need an "insider's" understanding and experience of relationships within that group. This is the group's shared, common heritage. It is part of a Tradition that changes but little over the years. It is the root of the group's identity. The greater part of this Tradition will remain unchanged in the next generation. It is from this Tradition that we need to draw the common idiom and the common grammar in which to communicate the Gospel today. Perhaps this is the only way in which communication is possible.

The Catechism, I contend, provides the *common idiom* and the *common grammar* for the faithful of today's church. It is through the Catechism that we can acquire a knowledge of the specifics that enable us to share in the faith community's culture. The liturgical action, as a celebration, provides the *insider's knowledge and experience of relationships.* What brings Catechism and celebration together is the gospel proclaimed as the *mirabilia Dei* (God's wonderful deeds) fulfilled today. "Today this Scripture has been fulfilled in your hearing" (Lk 4:21). "The Lord our God made a covenant with us in Horeb. Not with our fathers did the Lord make this covenant, but with us, who are all of us here alive this day" (Deut 5:2- 3). "What is this treachery which you have committed against the God of Israel in turning away this day from following the Lord, by building yourselves an altar this day in rebellion against the Lord?" (Jos 22:16). The appeal then is: "O that today you would hearken to his voice! Harden not your hearts, as at Meribah . . ." (Ps 95:7-8).

How do I suggest going about this? In preparing the homily, we read the gospel text and try to determine which areas of our life are addressed by the scriptural call. Is this call linked to some conceptual foundation or some doctrine? In our day this is almost always the case. What is the common idiom and grammar in which this is expressed? Here we can look to the Catechism. But we re-express this doctrine derived from the Catechism within the framework of the liturgical readings and as a call to faith and conversion, which in turn are expressed in commitment. In other words, we approach the Gospel with a question in mind. This question may concern what we remember, what we are presently celebrating, what we hope for, what commitment is expected of us.

As an example, let us use the First Sunday of Advent, Year B. The thread binding together the scattered pieces of tradition collected in the Gospel (Mk 13:33-37) is "And what I say to you, I say to all: Stay awake." Asleep, we are not on our guard. Awake, we are on guard. In other words, this gospel selection can be seen as a call for us to exercise our liberty in a responsible manner. From the tradition of catechetical teaching we can draw on the concepts of responsibility and imputability as presented in the Catechism (nos. 1731-1738) and present the meaning of these two terms according to our common idiom and grammar. We then look at the text with the help of a good commentary (e.g., *The New Jerome Biblical Commentary*). From the text we discover that the Gospel's call is not to say "Yes" to words, but to search for concrete forms in which our responsibility and imputability can show itself. Stay awake: be responsible; accept that both your actions and your omissions can be imputed to you. It is this form of discourse that is useful to those who may wish to refer to the common tradition. And, as the Catechism itself exhorts, we need to locate this tradition within the action of the liturgy.

The homilist can use the Catechism to discover a concept or an image within the common idiom of the church's catechetical tradition. In this key the homilist proposes the readings of the day as a call to faith and conversion. The liturgy, in its turn, integrates the response to the call within the action where the word proclaimed becomes the word actualized and celebrated.

Lectionary Readings and Catechism References

CYCLE A

1st Sunday of Advent

Lectionary (1)

Is. 2, 1-5
Ps. 121 (122), 1-2. 3-4. 4-5. 6-7. 8-9
Rom. 13, 11-14
Mt. 24, 37-44

Catechism

1020-1022: Particular judgment

2nd Sunday of Advent

Lectionary (4)

Is. 11, 1-10
Ps 71 (72), 1-2. 7-8. 12-13. 17
Rom. 15, 4-9
Lk. 3, 4. 6

Catechism

1739-1742: Human freedom in the plan of salvation

3rd Sunday of Advent

Lectionary (7)

Is. 35, 1-6. 10
Ps. 145 (146), 6-7. 8-9. 9-10
Jas. 5, 7-10
Mt. 11, 2-11

Catechism

456-460: Why the Word became flesh
547-550: Signs of the kingdom of God

4th Sunday of Advent

Lectionary (10)	Is. 7, 10-14
	Ps. 23 (24), 1-2. 3-4. 5-6
	Rom. 1, 1-7
	Mt. 1, 18-24
Catechism	1950-1964: Natural law and the law of the Old Testament

Christmas:
Mass at Midnight

Lectionary (14)	Is. 9, 1-6
	Ps. 95 (96), 1-2. 2-3. 11-12. 13
	Ti. 2, 11-14
	Lk 2, 1-14
Catechism	51-67: God's revelation through history climaxing in Jesus
	525-526: Jesus born in humility; the first witnesses

Christmas:
Mass at Dawn

Lectionary (15)	Is. 62. 11-12
	Ps. 96 (97) 1. 6. 11-12
	Ti. 3, 4-7
	Lk. 2. 15-20
Catechism	144-149: The obedience of faith

Christmas:
Mass during the Day

Lectionary (16)	Is. 52, 7-10
	Ps. 97 (98), 1. 2-3. 3-4. 5-6
	Heb. 1, 1-6
	Jn. 1-18 or 1-5. 9-14
Catechism	456-463: The Word became flesh

Sunday in the Octave of Christmas
Holy Family

Lectionary (17)	Sir. 3. 2-6. 12-14
	Ps. 127 (128). 1-2. 3. 4-5
	Col. 3, 12-21
	Mt. 2, 13-15. 19-23
Catechism	530: The flight into Egypt
	2196-2233: The fourth commandment

Octave of Christmas
Solemnity of Mary, Mother of God

Lectionary (18)	Nm. 6, 23-27
	Ps. 66 (67), 2-3. 5. 6. 8
	Gal. 4, 4-7
	Lk. 2, 16-21
Catechism	527: The Circumcision.
	484-487: Conceived of the Holy Spirit; born of the Virgin Mary

Epiphany

Lectionary (20)	Is. 60, 1-6
	Ps. 71 (72), 1-2. 7-8. 10-11. 12-13
	Eph. 3. 2-3. 5-6
	Mt. 2, 1-12
Catechism	528: Epiphany
	587-591: Jesus and the faith of Israel in One God and Saviour

Baptism of the Lord

Lectionary (21)	Is. 42, 1-4. 6-7
	Ps. 28 (29), 1-2. 3-4. 3. 9-10
	Acts 10, 34-38
	Mt. 3, 13-17
Catechism	1217-1228: Baptism in the economy of salvation

1st Sunday of Lent:

    Lectionary (22)   Gn. 2, 7-9; 3, 1-7
                               Ps. 50 (51), 3-4. 5-6. 12-13. 14, 17
                               Rom. 5, 12-19 or 5, 12. 17-19
                               Mt. 4, 1-11

    Catechism   538-540: The temptation of Jesus

2nd Sunday of Lent

    Lectionary (25)   Gn. 12, 1-4
                               Ps. 32 (33), 4-5. 18-19. 20. 22
                               2 Tm. 1, 8-10
                               Mt. 17, 1-9

    Catechism   554-556: Transfiguration
                               1023-1029: Heaven

3rd Sunday of Lent

    Lectionary (28)   Ex. 17, 3-7
                               Ps. 94 (95), 1-2. 6-7. 8-9
                               Rom. 5, 1-2. 5-8
                               Jn. 4, 5-42 or 4, 5-15. 19-26. 39. 40-42

    Catechism   1262-1274: The grace and effects of
                               baptism

4th Sunday of Lent

    Lectionary (31)   1 Sm. 16, 1. 6-7. 10-13
                               Ps. 22 (23), 1-3. 3-4. 5. 6
                               Eph 5, 8-14
                               Jn. 9, 1-41 or 9, 1. 6-9. 13-17. 34-38

    Catechism   1814-1816: Faith
                               1262-1274: The grace and effects of
                               baptism

5th Sunday of Lent

    Lectionary (34)   Ez. 37, 12-14
                                 Ps. 129 (130), 1-2. 3-4. 5-6. 7-8
                               Rom. 8. 8-11
                               Jn. 11, 1-45 or 11, 3-7. 17. 20-27. 33-45

    Catechism   651-655: The meaning and salvific
                               import of the resurrection

2nd Sunday of Easter
    Lectionary (43)   Acts 2, 42-47
                              Ps. 117 (118), 2-4. 13-15. 22-24
                              1 Pt. 1, 3-9
                              Jn. 20, 19-31
    Catechism   150-152: "I know in whom I
                              have believed."
                              446-451: Jesus is Lord.

3rd Sunday of Easter
    Lectionary (46)   Acts 2, 14. 22-28
                              Ps. 15 (16), 1-2. 5. 7-8. 9-10. 11
                              1 Pt. 1. 17-21
                              Lk. 24, 13-35

    Catechism   1084-1109: Christ and the Holy Spirit
                              in the liturgy
                              1373-1375: The presence of Jesus in the
                              eucharist by the power of his word
                              and the Holy Spirit

4th Sunday of Easter
    Lectionary (49)   Acts 2, 14. 36-41
                                Ps. 22 (23), 1-3. 3-4. 5. 6
                              1 Pt. 2, 20-25
                              Jn. 10, 1-10

    Catechism   1539-1553: The sacrament of orders in
                                the economy of salvation

5th Sunday of Easter
    Lectionary (52)   Acts 6, 1-7
                                Ps. 32 (33), 1-2. 4-5. 18-19
                              1 Pt. 2, 4-9
                              Jn. 14, 1-12

    Catechism   2259-2283: Respect for human life

6th Sunday of Easter

Lectionary (55)	Acts 8, 5-8. 14-17 Ps. 65 (66), 1-3. 4-5. 6-7. 16. 20 1 Pt. 3, 15-18 Jn. 14, 15-21
Catechism	727-730: The Holy Spirit brings the work of Jesus to completion. 1285-1314: Confirmation in the economy of salvation

Ascension

Lectionary (58)	Acts 1, 1-11 Ps. 46 (47), 2-3. 6-7. 8-9 Eph. 1, 17-23 Mt. 28, 16-20
Catechism	659-664: Jesus ascended to the right hand of the Father.

Pentecost

Lectionary (63)	Acts 2, 1-11 Ps. 103 (104), 1. 24. 29-30. 31. 34 1 Cor. 12, 3-7. 12-13 Jn. 20, 19-23
Catechism	731-741: The Holy Spirit and the church of the "Last" times

Trinity Sunday

Lectionary (164)	Ex. 34, 4-6. 8-9 Dn. 3, 52. 53. 54. 55. 56 2 Cor. 13, 11-13 Jn. 3, 16-18
Catechism	1077-1083: The Father as the source and goal of the liturgy 1243-1244: "Mystagogy" of the rites of initiation

Sunday after Trinity Sunday
Corpus Christi

Lectionary (167)	Dt. 8, 2-3. 14-16
	Ps. 147, 12-13. 14-15. 19-20
	1 Cor. 10, 16-17
	Jn. 6, 51-58
Catechism	1382-1389: The eucharist as paschal meal

2nd Sunday in Ordinary Time

Lectionary (64)	Is. 49, 3. 5-6
	Ps. 39 (40), 2. 4. 7-8. 8-9. 10
	1 Cor. 1, 1-3
	Jn. 1, 29-34
Catechism	386-389: Where sin has abounded, grace has abounded more.

3rd Sunday in Ordinary Time

Lectionary (67)	Is. 8, 23-9,3
	Ps. 26 (27), 1. 4. 13-14
	1 Cor. 1, 10-13. 17
	Mt. 4, 12-23 or 4, 12-17
Catechism	200-227: God's self revelation; the implication of faith in one God

4th Sunday in Ordinary Time

Lectionary (70)	Zep. 2, 3; 3, 12-13
	Ps. 145 (146), 6-7. 8-9. 9-10
	1 Cor. 1, 26-31
	Mt. 5, 1-12
Catechism	1716-1724: Christian happiness

5th Sunday in Ordinary Time

Lectionary (73)	Is. 58, 7-10
	Ps. 111 (112), 4-5. 6-7. 8-9
	1 Cor. 2, 1-5
	Mt. 5, 13-16
Catechism	2493-2499: Use of the means of social communication
	2500-2503: Truth, beauty, and sacred art

6th Sunday in Ordinary Time
    Lectionary (76)   Sir. 15, 15-20
        Ps. 118 (119), 1-2. 4-5. 17-18. 33-34
        1 Cor. 2, 6-10
        Mt. 5, 17-37 or 5, 20-22. 27-28. 33-34. 37

    Catechism   1965-1974: The new law or the evangelical law
        2044-2046: Moral life and missionary witness
        2514-2527: Purity of heart (ninth Commandment)

7th Sunday in Ordinary Time
    Lectionary (79)   LPs. 102 (103), 1-2. 3-4. 8. 10. 12-13
        1 Cor. 3, 16-23
        Mt. 5, 38-48

    Catechism   2284-2301: Respect for personal dignity

8th Sunday in Ordinary Time
    Lectionary (82)   Is. 49, 14-15
        Ps. 61 (62), 2-3. 6-7. 8-9
        1 Cor. 4, 1-5
        Mt. 6, 24-34

    Catechism   302-314: God realizes the divine plan: God's providence
        2828-2837: Give us this day our daily bread.

9th Sunday in Ordinary Time
    Lectionary (85)   Dt. 11, 18. 26-28
        Ps. 30 (31), 2-3. 3-4. 17. 25
        Rom. 3, 21-25. 28
        Mt. 7, 21-27

    Catechism   2012-2016: Christian holiness

10th Sunday in Ordinary Time

Lectionary (88)	Hos. 6, 3-6
	Ps. 49 (50), 1. 8. 12-13. 14-15
	Rom. 4, 18-25
	Mt. 9, 9-13
Catechism	1846-1848: Mercy and sin

11th Sunday in Ordinary Time

Lectionary (91)	Ex. 19, 2-6
	Ps. 99 (100), 1-2. 3. 5
	Rom. 5, 6-11
	Mt. 9, 36 - 10, 8
Catechism	1554-1571: Degrees of Orders in the church

12th Sunday in Ordinary Time

Lectionary (94)	Jer. 20, 10-13
	Ps. 68 (69), 8-10. 14. 17. 33-35
	Rom. 5, 12-15
	Mt. 10, 26-33
Catechism	1030-1032: Purgatory
	1033-1037: Hell

13th Sunday in Ordinary Time

Lectionary (97)	2 Kgs. 4, 8-11. 14-16
	Ps. 88 (89), 2-3. 16-17. 18-19
	Rom. 6, 3-4. 8-11
	Mt. 10, 37-42
Catechism	897-913: Laity: their participation in Christ's threefold mission

14th Sunday in Ordinary Time

Lectionary (100)	Zec. 9, 9-10
	Ps. 144 (145), 1-2. 8-9. 10-11. 13-14
	Rom. 8, 9. 11-13
	Mt. 11, 25-30
Catechism	2786-2793: Our Father

15th Sunday in Ordinary Time

Lectionary (103)	Is. 55, 10-11
	Ps. 64 (65), 10. 11. 12-13. 14
	Rom. 8, 18-23
	Mt. 13, 1-23 or 13, 1-9
Catechism	1987-2011: Justification, grace, merit

16th Sunday in Ordinary Time

Lectionary (106)	Wis. 12, 13. 16-19
	Ps. 85 (86) 5-6. 9-10. 15-16
	Rom. 8, 26-27
	Mt. 13, 24-43 or 13, 24-30
Catechism	163-165: Faith as the beginning of eternal life
	583-586: Jesus and the temple

17th Sunday in Ordinary Time

Lectionary (109)	1 Kgs. 3, 5. 7-12
	Ps. 118 (119), 57, 72, 76-77, 127-128. 129-130
	Rom. 8, 28-30
	Mt. 13, 44-52 or 13, 44-46
Catechism	2822-2827: Thy will be done on earth as it is in heaven.

18th Sunday in Ordinary Time

Lectionary (112)	Is. 55, 1-3
	Ps. 144 (145), 8-9. 15-16. 17-18
	Rom. 8, 35. 37-39
	Mt. 14, 13-21
Catechism	1878-1885: The communitarian character of the human vocation

19th Sunday in Ordinary Time

Lectionary (115)	1 Kgs. 19, 9. 11-13
	Ps. 84 (85), 9. 10. 11-12. 13-14
	Rom. 9, 1-5
	Mt. 14, 22-33
Catechism	168-169: "Look on the faith of your church."

20th Sunday in Ordinary Time

Lectionary (118)	Is. 56, 1. 6-7
	Ps. 66 (67), 2-3. 5. 6. 8
	Rom. 11, 13-15. 29-32
	Mt. 15, 21-28
Catechism	170-171: The language of faith

21st Sunday in Ordinary Time

Lectionary (121)	Is. 22, 15. 19-23
	Ps. 137 (138), 1-2. 2-3. 6. 8
	Rom. 11, 33-36
	Mt. 16, 13-20
Catechism	172-175: Only one faith through the centuries

22nd Sunday in Ordinary Time

Lectionary (124)	Jer. 20, 7-9
	Ps. 62 (63) 2, 3-4. 5-6. 8-9
	Rom. 12, 1-2
	Mt. 16, 21-27
Catechism	2084-2094: Thou shalt adore the Lord thy God.

23rd Sunday in Ordinary Time

Lectionary (127)	Ez. 33, 7-9
	Ps. 94 (95), 1-2. 6-7. 8-9
	Rom. 13, 8-10
	Mt. 18, 15-20
Catechism	1886-1889: Conversion and society

24th Sunday in Ordinary Time

Lectionary (130)	Sir. 27, 30 - 28, 7
	Ps. 102 (103), 1-2. 3-4. 9-10. 11-12
	Rom. 14, 7-9
	Mt. 18, 21-35
Catechism	2838-2845: Forgive us our sins as we forgive those who sin against us.

25th Sunday in Ordinary Time

Lectionary (133)   Is. 55, 6-9

                        Ps. 144 (145), 2-3. 8-9. 17-18

                        Phil. 1, 20-24, 27

                        Mt. 20, 1-16

Catechism   1996-2005: Grace

26th Sunday in Ordinary Time

Lectionary (136)   Ez. 18, 25-28

                        Ps. 24 (25), 4-5. 6-7. 8-9

                        Phil. 2, 1-11 or 2, 1-5

                        Mt. 21, 28-32

Catechism   2006-2011: Merit

27th Sunday in Ordinary Time

Lectionary (139)   Is. 5, 1-7

                        Ps. 79 (80), 9. 12. 13-14. 15-16. 19-20

                        Phil. 4, 6-9

                        Mt. 21, 33-43

Catechism   2816-2821: Thy kingdom come.

28th Sunday in Ordinary Time

Lectionary (142)   Is. 25, 6-10

                        Ps. 22 (23), 1-3. 3-4. 5. 6

                        Phil. 4, 12-14. 19-20

                        Mt. 22, 1-14 or 22, 1-10

Catechism   2535-2543: Covetousness versus the desires of the Spirit

29th Sunday in Ordinary Time

Lectionary (145)   Is. 45, 1. 4-6

                        Ps. 95 (96), 1. 3. 4-5. 7-8. 9-10

                        1 Thes., 1. 1-5

                        Mt. 22, 15-21

Catechism   2234-2246: Authority in civil society

                        356-368: Created in God's image (what has to be rendered to God)

30th Sunday in Ordinary Time
Lectionary (148)	Ex. 22, 20-26
	Ps. 17 (18), 2-3. 3-4. 47. 51
	1 Thes. 1, 5-10
	Mt. 22, 34-40
Catechism	1822-1829: Charity

31st Sunday in Ordinary Time
Lectionary (151)	Mal. 1, 14 - 2, 2. 8-10
	Ps. 130 (131), 1. 2. 3
	1 Thes. 2, 7-9. 13
	Mt. 23, 1-12
Catechism	2095-2109: Thou shalt worship the Lord alone.

32nd Sunday in Ordinary Time
Lectionary (154)	Wis. 6, 12-16
	Ps. 62 (63), 2. 3-4. 5-6. 7-8
	1 Thes. 4, 13-18 or 4, 13-14
	Mt. 25, 1-13
Catechism	914-933: Consecrated life in the church
	1618-1620: Virginity for the kingdom

33rd Sunday in Ordinary Time
Lectionary (157)	Prv. 31, 10-13. 19-20. 30-31
	Ps. 127 (128), 1-2. 3. 4-5
	1 Thes. 5, 1-6
	Mt. 25, 14-30 or 25, 14-15. 19-20
Catechism	946-959: The communion of saints

Last Sunday in Ordinary Time
Christ the King
Lectionary (160)	Ez. 34, 11-12. 15-17
	Ps. 22 (23), 1-2. 2-3. 5-6
	1 Cor. 15, 20-26. 28
	Mt. 25, 31-46
Catechism	668-679: He will come in glory to judge the living and the dead.

CYCLE B

1st Sunday of Advent

    Lectionary (2)
        Is. 63, 16-17. 19; 64, 2-7
        Ps. 79 (80), 2-3. 15-16. 18-19
        1 Cor. 1, 3-9
        Mk. 13, 33-37

    Catechism
        1731-1738: Responsibility and imputability

2nd Sunday of Advent

    Lectionary (5)
        Is. 40, 1-5. 9-11
        Ps. 84 (85), 9-10. 11-12. 13-14
        2 Pt. 3, 8-14
        Mk. 1, 1-8

    Catechism
        1739-1742: Freedom and sin; obstacles to freedom, freedom and salvation; freedom and grace

3rd Sunday of Advent

    Lectionary (8)
        Is. 61, 1-2. 10-11
        Lk. 1, 46-48. 49-50. 53-54
        1 Thes. 5, 16-24
        Jn. 1, 6-8. 19-28

    Catechism
        759-769: The role of John the Baptist

4th Sunday of Advent
    Lectionary (11)   2 Sm. 7, 1-5. 8-11. 16
                             Ps. 88 (89), 2-3. 4-5. 27. 29
                             Rom. 16, 25-27
                             Lk. 1, 26-38

    Catechism   464-469: Jesus, true God and true human person.

Christmas:
Mass at Midnight
    Lectionary (14)   Is. 9, 1-6
                             Ps. 95 (96), 1-2. 2-3. 11-12. 13
                             Ti. 1, 11-14
                             Lk. 2, 10-14

    Catechism   461-463: The Incarnation

Christmas:
Mass at Dawn
    Lectionary (15)   Is. 62, 11-12
                               Ps. 96 (97), 1. 6. 11-12
                             Ti. 3, 4-7
                             Lk. 2, 15-20

    Catechism   461-463: The Incarnation

Christmas:
Mass during the Day
    Lectionary (16)   Is. 51, 7-10
                               Ps. 97 (98), 1. 2-3. 3-4. 5-6
                             Heb. 1, 1-6
                             Jn. 1, 1-18 or 1-5. 9-14

    Catechism   461-463: The Incarnation

Sunday in the Octave of Christmas
Holy Family

Lectionary (17)	Sir. 3, 2-6. 12-14
	Ps. 127 (128), 1-2. 3. 4-5
	Col. 3, 12-21
	Lk 2, 22-40 or 2, 22. 39-40
Catechism	529: Presentation of the Child Jesus in the temple
	2214-2233: Duties of the members of the family; the family and the Kingdom

Octave of Christmas
Solemnity of Mary, Mother of God

Lectionary (18)	Nm. 6, 22-27
	Ps. 66 (67), 2-3. 5. 6. 8
	Gal. 4, 4-7
	Lk. 2, 16-21
Catechism	495; 502: Divine maternity, virginal maternity in the plan of God

Epiphany

Lectionary (20)	Is. 60, 1-6
	Ps. 71 (72), 1-2. 7-8. 10-11. 12-13
	Eph. 3, 2-3. 5-6
	Mt. 2, 1-12
Catechism	528: The epiphany manifesting Jesus as Messiah of Israel, Son of God, and Saviour of the world

Baptism of the Lord

Lectionary (21)	Is. 42, 1-4. 6-7
	Ps. 28 (29), 1-2. 3-4. 3. 9-10
	Acts 10, 34-38
	Mk. 1, 7-11
Catechism	535-537: The baptism of Jesus
	1223-1225: The baptism of Jesus in the economy of salvation
	1226-1228: Baptism in the church

1st Sunday of Lent

Lectionary (23)

Gn. 9, 8-15
Ps. 24 (25), 4-5. 6-7. 8-9
1 Pt. 3, 18-22
Mk. 1, 12-15

Catechism

309-314: Providence and the stumbling
block of evil
2110-2159: "No other gods before me";
the name Christian

2nd Sunday of Lent

Lectionary (26)

Gn. 22, 1-2. 9. 10-13. 15-18
Ps. 115 (116), 10. 15. 16-17. 18-19
Rom. 8, 31-34
Mk. 9, 2-10

Catechism

101-108: Christ, the unique word, the
inspiration and truth of Scripture
131-133: Scripture in the life of the
church

3rd Sunday of Lent

Lectionary (29)

Ex. 20, 1-17 or 20, 1-3. 7-8. 12-17
Ps. 18 (19), 8. 9. 10. 11
1 Cor. 1, 22-25
Jn. 2, 13-25

Catechism

583-586: Jesus and the temple
797-798: The church - temple of the
Holy Spirit

4th Sunday of Lent

Lectionary (32)

2 Chr. 36, 14-17. 19-23
Ps. 136 (137), 1-2. 3. 4-5. 6
Eph. 2, 4-10
Jn. 3, 14-21

Catechism

595-598: The authorities and the death
of Jesus
599-605: The redemptive death of Jesus
in the plan of salvation

5th Sunday of Lent

Lectionary (35)   Jer. 31, 31-34
                               Ps. 50 (51), 3-4. 12-13. 14-15
                               Heb. 5, 7-9
                               Jn. 12, 20-33

Catechism   606-618: Jesus offers himself to the
                               Father for our sins

2nd Sunday of Easter

Lectionary (44)   Acts 4, 32-35
                               Ps. 117 (118), 2-4. 13-15. 22-24
                               1 Jn. 5, 1-6
                               Jn. 20, 19-31

Catechism   651-655: Meaning and salvific import
                               of the Resurrection

3rd Sunday of Easter

Lectionary (47)   Acts 3, 13-15. 17-19
                               Ps. 4, 2. 4. 7-8. 9
                               1 Jn. 2, 1-5
                               Lk. 24, 35-48

Catechism   645-646: The risen humanity of Jesus

4th Sunday of Easter

Lectionary (50)   Acts 4, 8-12
                               Ps. 117 (118), 1. 8-9. 21-23. 26. 21. 29
                               1 Jn. 3, 1-2
                               Jn. 10, 11-18

Catechism   857-896: The church is apostolic - built
                               on the foundation of the apostles; role
                               of the hierarchy

5th Sunday of Easter

Lectionary (53)   Acts 9, 26-31
                               Ps. 21 (22), 26-27. 28. 30. 31-32
                               1 Jn. 3, 18-24
                               Jn. 15, 1-8

Catechism   771-801: The church as visible and
                               spiritual; the universal sacrament of
                               salvation; charisms

6th Sunday of Easter

Lectionary (56)

Acts 10, 25-26. 34-35. 44-48
Ps. 97 (98), 1. 2-3. 3-4
1 Jn. 4, 7-10
Jn. 15, 9-17

Catechism

1878-1889: Communitarian character
of the human vocation

Ascension

Lectionary (58)

Acts 1, 1-11
Ps. 46 (47), 2-3. 6-7. 8-9
Eph. 1, 17-23
Mt. 28, 16-20

Catechism

737-741: The Holy Spirit and the church

Pentecost Sunday

Lectionary (63)

Acts 2, 1-11
Ps. 103 (104), 1. 24. 29-30. 31. 34
1 Cor. 12, 3-7. 12-13
Jn. 20, 19-23

Catechism

702-716: The Holy Spirit - a spirit of
renewal

Sunday after Pentecost
Trinity Sunday   ˙

Lectionary (165)

Dt. 4, 32-34, 39-40
Ps. 32 (33), 4-5. 6. 9. 18-19. 20. 22
Rom. 8, 14-17
Mt. 28, 16-20

Catechism

232-248: The revelation of God as
Trinity

Sunday after Trinity Sunday
Corpus Christi

Lectionary (168)

Ex. 24, 3-8
Ps. 115 (116), 12-13. 15-16. 17-18
Heb. 9, 11-15

Catechism

1333-1336: The eucharist in the plan of
salvation

2nd Sunday in Ordinary Time

Lectionary (65) 1 Sm. 3, 3-10. 19
Ps. 39 (40), 2. 4. 7-8. 8-9. 10
1 Cor. 6, 13-15. 17-20
Jn 1, 35-42

Catechism 27-43: Our capacity for God, our desire for God, the knowledge of God in the church

3rd Sunday in Ordinary Time

Lectionary (68) Jon. 3, 1-5. 10
Ps. 24 (25), 4-5. 6-7. 8-9
1 Cor. 7, 29-31
Mk. 1, 14-20

Catechism 144-165: "I believe" - the obedience of faith and the characteristics of faith

4th Sunday in Ordinary Time

Lectionary (71) Dt. 18, 15-20
Ps. 94 (95), 1-2. 6-7. 7-9
1 Cor. 7, 32-35
Mk. 1, 21-28

Catechism 391-395: Fall of the angels
1042-1050: The new heaven and the new earth

5th Sunday in Ordinary Time

Lectionary (74) Jb. 7, 1-4. 6-7
Ps. 146 (147), 1-2. 3-4. 5-6
1 Cor. 9, 16-19. 22-23
Mk. 1, 29-39

Catechism 1499-1523: Prayer and healing in the anointing of the sick

6th Sunday in Ordinary Time

Lectionary (77)   Lv. 13, 1-2. 44-46
                      Ps. 31 (32), 1-2. 5. 11
                      1 Cor. 10, 31 - 11,1
                      Mk. 1, 40-45

Catechism   1897-1904: Authority

7th Sunday in Ordinary Time

Lectionary (80)   Is. 43, 18-19. 21-22. 24-25
                      Ps. 40 (41), 2-3. 4-5. 13-14
                      2 Cor. 1, 18-22
                      Mk. 2, 1-12

Catechism   1450-1460: Acts of the penitent and the
                      forgiveness of sins (sacrament of
                      reconciliation)

8th Sunday in Ordinary Time

Lectionary (83)   Hos. 2, 16-17. 21-22
                      Ps. 102 (103), 1-2. 3-4. 8. 10. 12-13
                      2 Cor. 3, 1-6
                      Mk. 2, 18-22

Catechism   2084-2094: The God we know in the
                      first commandment

9th Sunday in Ordinary Time

Lectionary (86)   Dt. 11, 18. 26-28
                      Ps. 30 (31), 2-3. 3-4. 17. 25
                      Rom. 3, 21-25, 28
                      Mt. 7, 21-27

Catechism   2168-2188: The Sabbath
                      (third commandment)

10th Sunday in Ordinary Time

Lectionary (89)   Gn 3, 9-15
                      Ps. 129 (130), 1-2. 3-4. 5-6. 7-8
                      2 Cor. 4, 13 - 5, 1
                      Mk. 3, 20-35

Catechism   1846-1869: God's mercy is always
                      there; but sin and its proliferation are
                      realities

11th Sunday in Ordinary Time

Lectionary (92)	Ez. 17, 22-24
	Ps. 91 (92), 2-3. 13-14. 15-16
	2 Cor. 5, 6-10
	Mk. 4, 26-34
Catechism	751-757: Names and images of the church

12th Sunday in Ordinary Time

Lectionary (95)	Jb. 38, 1. 8-11
	Ps. 106 (107), 23-24. 25-26. 28-29. 30-31
	2 Cor. 5, 14-17
	Mk. 4, 35-41
Catechism	1762-1770: The passion; the passions and moral life

13th Sunday in Ordinary Time

Lectionary (98)	Wis. 1, 13-15; 2, 23-24
	Ps. 29 (30), 2. 4. 5-6. 11. 12. 13
	2 Cor. 8. 7. 9. 13-15
	Mk. 5, 21-43 or 5, 21-24, 35-43
Catechism	1113-1130: Sacraments of Christ; sacraments of faith; sacraments of salvation

14th Sunday in Ordinary Time

Lectionary (101)	Ez. 2, 2-5
	Ps. 122 (123), 1-2. 3-4
	2 Cor. 12, 7-10
	Mk. 6, 1-6
Catechism	153-165: Characteristics of faith

15th Sunday in Ordinary Time

Lectionary (104)	Am. 7, 12-15
	Ps. 84 (85), 9-10. 11-12. 13-14
	Eph. 1, 3-14 or 1, 3-10
	Mk 6, 7-13
Catechism	830-856: The church is catholic; mission is a consequence

16th Sunday in Ordinary Time
Lectionary (107)   Jer. 23, 1-6
                      Ps. 22 (23), 1-3. 3-4. 5. 6
                      Eph. 2, 13-18
                      Mk. 6, 30-34

Catechism   1750-1756: Sources of morality
                      2030-2051: The church as mother and
                      educatrix in the area of morality

17th Sunday in Ordinary Time
Lectionary (110)   2 Kgs. 4, 42-44
                      Ps. 144 (145), 10-11. 15-16. 17-18
                      Eph. 4, 1-6
                      Jn. 6, 1-15

Catechism   1382-1390: The eucharist as paschal
                      meal

18th Sunday in Ordinary Time
Lectionary (113)   Ex. 16, 2-4. 12-15
                      Ps. 77 (78), 3-4. 23-24. 25. 54
                      Eph. 4, 17. 20-24
                      Jn. 6, 24-35

Catechism   1391-1401: Fruits of eucharistic com
                      munion and the commitment it entails
                      1524-1525: Viaticum as the last sacra-
                      ment of the Christian

19th Sunday in Ordinary Time
Lectionary (116)   1 Kgs. 19, 4-8
                      Ps. 33 (34), 2-3. 4-5. 6-7. 8-9
                      Eph. 4, 30 - 5, 2
                      Jn. 6, 41-51

Catechism   1402-1405: Eucharist as pledge of
                      eternal life

20th Sunday in Ordinary Time
Lectionary (119)   Prv. 9, 1-6
                        Ps. 33 (34), 2-3. 10-11. 12-13. 14-15
                        Eph. 5, 15-20
                        Jn. 6, 51-58

Catechism   1324-1327: Eucharist as source and
                        summit of the church's life

21st Sunday in Ordinary Time
Lectionary (122)   Jos. 24, 1-2. 15-17. 18
                        Ps. 33 (34), 2-3. 16-17. 18-19. 20-21.
                        22-23
                        Eph. 5, 21-32
                        Jn. 6, 60-69

Catechism   1333-1336: The signs of bread and wine
                        and the new meaning given them

22nd Sunday in Ordinary Time
Lectionary (125)   Dt. 4, 1-2. 6-8
                        Ps. 14 (15), 2-3. 3-4. 4-5
                        Jas. 1, 17-18. 21-22. 27
                        Mk. 7, 1-8. 14-15. 21-23

Catechism   1776-1794: The moral conscience
                        84-95: Interpreting the heritage of
                        faith

23rd Sunday in Ordinary Time
Lectionary (128)   Is. 35, 4-7
                        Ps. 145 (146), 7. 8-9. 9-10
                        Jas. 2, 1-5
                        Mk. 7, 31-37

Catechism   2464-2474: To live in the truth; to bear
                        witness to the truth

24th Sunday in Ordinary Time

Lectionary (131)	Is. 50, 4-9
	Ps. 114 (115), 1-2. 3-4. 5-6. 8-9
	Jas. 2, 14-18
	Mk. 8, 27-35
Catechism	599-605: Christ's redemptive death in the divine plan of salvation

25th Sunday in Ordinary Time

Lectionary (134)	Wis. 2, 12. 17-20
	Ps. 53 (54), 3-4. 5. 6-8
	Jas. 3, 16 - 4, 3
	Mk. 9, 30-37
Catechism	1929-1938: Respect for human persons; differences among people

26th Sunday in Ordinary Time

Lectionary (137)	Nm. 11, 25-29
	Ps. 18 (19), 8. 10. 12-13. 14
	Jas. 5, 1-6
	Mk. 9, 38-43. 45. 47-48
Catechism	1939-1942: Human solidarity

27th Sunday in Ordinary Time

Lectionary (140)	Gn. 2, 18-24
	Ps. 127 (128), 1-2. 3. 4-5. 6
	Heb. 2, 9-11
	Mk. 10, 2-16 or 10, 2-12
Catechism	1602-1617: Marriage in the plan of God
	1643-1654: The demands of conjugal love
	369-373: Male and female he created them

28th Sunday in Ordinary Time

Lectionary (143)   Wis. 7, 7-11
Ps. 89 (90), 12-13. 14-15. 16-17
Heb. 4, 12-13
Mk. 10, 17-30 or 10, 17-27

Catechism   2402-2406: The universal destination of goods and private property

29th Sunday in Ordinary Time

Lectionary (146)   Is. 53, 10-11
Ps. 32 (33), 4-5. 18-19. 20. 22
Heb. 4, 14-16
Mk. 10, 35-45 or 10, 42-45

Catechism   1905-1917: Common good; responsibility and participation

30th Sunday in Ordinary Time

Lectionary (149)   Jer. 31, 7-9
Ps. 125 (126), 1-2. 2-3. 4-5. 6
Heb. 5, 1-6
Mk. 10, 46-52

Catechism   430-435: Jesus (the meaning and significance of the name)

31st Sunday in Ordinary Time

Lectionary (152)   Dt. 6, 2-6
Ps. 17 (18), 2-3. 3-4. 47. 51
Heb. 7, 23-28
Mk. 12, 28-34

Catechism   1822-1829: Charity

32nd Sunday in Ordinary Time

Lectionary (155)   1 Kgs. 17, 10-16
Ps. 146, 7. 8-9. 9-10
Heb. 9, 24-28
Mk. 12, 38-44 or 12, 41-44

Catechism   2443-2449: Love for the poor

33rd Sunday in Ordinary Time

    Lectionary (158)   Dn. 12, 1-3
                                      Ps. 16, 5. 8. 9-10. 11
                                      Heb. 10, 11-14. 18
                                      Mk. 13, 24-32

    Catechism   1038-1041: The Last Judgment

Last Sunday in Ordinary Time
Christ the King

    Lectionary (161)   Dn. 7, 13-14
                                        Ps. 92 (93), 1. 1-2. 5
                                      Rv. 1, 5-8
                                        Jn. 18, 33-37

    Catechism   2471-2492: Bearing witness to the truth; respect for the truth; offences against the truth

CYCLE C

1st Sunday of Advent

    Lectionary (3)   Jer. 33, 14-16
                               Ps. 24 (25), 4-5. 8-9. 10. 14
                               1 Thes 3, 12 - 4, 2
                               Lk 21, 25-28. 34-36

    Catechism   2846-2854: Lead us not into temptation; but deliver us from evil

2nd Sunday of Advent

    Lectionary (6)   Bar. 5, 1-9
                               Ps. 125 (126), 1-2. 2-3. 4-5. 6
                               Phil. 1, 4-6. 8-11
                               Lk. 3, 1-6

    Catechism   717-720: John: Precursor, prophet, baptizer

3rd Sunday of Advent

    Lectionary (9)   Zep. 3, 14-18
                                 Is. 12, 2-3. 4, 5-6
                               Phil. 4, 4-7
                               Lk. 3, 10-18

    Catechism   2822-2827: Thy will be done on earth as it is in heaven

4th Sunday of Advent

    Lectionary (12)   Mi. 5, 1-4
                                    Ps. 79 (80), 2-3. 15-16. 18-19
                                    Heb. 10. 5-10
                                    Lk. 1, 39-45

    Catechism   721-726: Rejoice! You are full of grace

Christmas:
Mass at Midnight

    Lectionary (14)   Is. 9, 1-6
                                      Ps. 95 (96), 1-2. 2-3. 11-12. 13
                                    Ti. 2, 11-14
                                    Lk. 2, 1-14

    Catechism   525: The mystery of Christmas

Christmas:
Mass at Dawn

    Lectionary (15)   Is. 62, 11-12
                                      Ps. 96 (97), 1. 6. 11-12
                                    Ti. 3, 4-7
                                    Lk. 2, 15-20

    Catechism   525: The mystery of Christmas

Christmas:
Mass during the Day

    Lectionary (16)   Is. 52, 7-10
                                      Ps. 97 (98), 1. 2-3. 3-4. 5-6
                                    Heb. 1, 1-6
                                    Jn. 1, 1-8 or 1-5, 9-14

    Catechism   525: The mystery of Christmas

Sunday in the Octave of Christmas
Holy Family

Lectionary (17)	Sir. 3, 2-6. 12-14
	Ps. 127 (128), 1-2. 3. 4-5
	Col. 3, 12-21
	Lk. 2, 41-52
Catechism	2234-2243: Living in the earthly city: the role of authority
	1655-1658: The family as the domestic church
	2232-2233: The family and the kingdom

Octave of Christmas
Solemnity of Mary, Mother of God

Lectionary (18)	Nm. 6, 22-27
	Ps. 66 (67), 2-3. 5. 6. 8
	Gal. 4, 4-7
	Lk. 2, 16-21
Catechism	964-970: Mary - Mother of the church

Epiphany

Lectionary (20)	Is. 60, 1-6
	Ps. 71 (72), 1-2. 7-8. 10-11. 12-13
	Eph. 3, 2-3. 5-6
	Mt. 2, 1-12
Catechism	512-519: The mysteries of Jesus and our communion in these mysteries

Baptism of the Lord

Lectionary (21)	Is. 42. 1-4. 6-7
	Ps. 28 (29), 1-2. 3-4. 3. 9-10
	Acts 10, 34-38
	Lk. 3, 15-16. 21-22
Catechism	535-537: The baptism of Jesus

1st Sunday of Lent

Lectionary (24)   Dt. 26, 4-10
                       Ps. 90 (91), 1-2. 10-11. 12-13. 14-15
                       Rom. 10, 8-13
                       Lk. 4, 1-13

Catechism   2846-2854: Lead us not into tempta-
                       tion; but deliver us from evil

2nd Sunday of Lent

Lectionary (27)   Gn. 15, 5-12. 17-18
                       Ps. 26 (27), 1. 7-8. 8-9. 13-14
                       Phil. 3, 17 - 4, 1 or 3, 20 - 4, 1
                       Lk. 9, 28-36

Catechism   516-521: Characteristics common to
                       the mysteries of Jesus; our
                       communion in the mysteries of Jesus
                       1817-1821: Hope

3rd Sunday of Lent

Lectionary (30)   Ex. 3, 1-8, 13-15
                       Ps. 102 (103), 1-2. 3-4. 6-7. 8. 11
                       1 Cor. 10, 1-6. 10-12
                       Lk. 13, 1-9

Catechism   541-546: The Kingdom is near;
                       proclaiming the Kingdom

4th Sunday of Lent

Lectionary (33)   Jos. 5, 9. 10-12
                       Ps. 33 (34), 2-3. 4-5. 6-7
                       2 Cor. 5, 17-21
                       Lk. 15, 1-3. 11-32

Catechism   1427-1449: Conversion; interior
                       repentance; the many forms of
                       penitential practice in the church

5th Sunday of Lent

Lectionary (36)

Is. 43, 16-21
Ps. 125 (126), 1-2. 2-3. 4-5. 6
Phil. 3, 8-14
Jn. 8, 1-11

Catechism

577-582: Jesus and the Law
2331-2391: The sixth commandment

2nd Sunday of Easter

Lectionary (45)

Acts 5, 12-16
Ps. 117 (118), 2-4. 13-15. 22-24
Rv. 1, 9-11. 12-13. 17-19
Jn. 20, 19-31

Catechism

153-165: Characteristics of faith
441-445: Jesus, the only begotten Son
of God

3rd Sunday of Easter

Lectionary (48)

Acts 5, 27-32. 40-41
Ps. 29 (30), 2. 4. 5-6. 11-12. 13
Rv. 5, 11-14
Jn. 21, 1-19 or 21, 1-14

Catechism

641-644: Apparitions of the Risen One

4th Sunday of Easter

Lectionary (51)

Acts 13, 14. 43-52
Ps. 99 (100), 1-2. 3. 5
Rv. 7, 9. 14-17
Jn. 10, 27-30

Catechism

410-412: God has not abandoned the
human race to the power of death
(after the Fall)

5th Sunday of Easter

Lectionary (54)

Acts 14, 21-27
Ps. 145, 8-9. 10-11. 12-13
Rv. 21, 1-5
Jn. 13, 31-33. 34-35

Catechism

1822-1829: Charity
1396-1401: The eucharist and unity

6th Sunday of Easter
    Lectionary (57)

Acts 15, 1-2. 22-29
Ps. 66 (67), 2-3. 5. 6. 8
Rv. 21, 10-14. 22-23
Jn. 14, 23-29

    Catechism

731-732: The Holy Spirit and the "last" times

Ascension
    Lectionary (58)

Acts 1, 1-11
Ps. 46 (47), 2-3. 6-7. 8-9
Eph. 1, 17-23
Mt. 28, 16-20

    Catechism

668-679: He will come again to judge the living and the dead

Pentecost Sunday
    Lectionary (63)

Acts 2, 1-11
Ps. 103 (104), 1. 24. 29-30. 31. 34
1 Cor. 12, 3-7. 12-13
Jn. 20, 19-23

    Catechism

1830-1831: The gifts and fruits of the Holy Spirit

Sunday after Pentecost
Trinity Sunday
    Lectionary (166)

Prv. 8, 22-31
Ps. 8, 4-5. 6-7. 8-9
Rom. 5, 1-5
Jn. 16, 12-15

    Catechism

1077-1109: Liturgy: work of the Trinity
109-119: The Holy Spirit, interpreter of the Scripture
249-260: Formation of the doctrine of the Trinity and trinitarian missions

Sunday after Trinity Sunday
Corpus Christi

Lectionary (169)

Gn. 14, 18-20
Ps. 109 (110), 1. 2. 3. 4
1 Cor. 11, 23-26
Lk. 9, 11-17

Catechism

1373-1381: Christ's presence (in the eucharist) by the power of his word and the Holy Spirit

2nd Sunday in Ordinary Time

Lectionary (66)

Is. 62, 1-5
Ps. 95 (96), 1-2. 2-3. 7-8. 9-10
1 Cor. 12, 4-11
Jn. 2, 1-12

Catechism

422-429: Christ at the heart of catechesis

3rd Sunday in Ordinary Time

Lectionary (69)

Neh. 8, 2-4. 5-6. 8-10
Ps. 18 (19), 8. 9. 10. 15
1 Cor. 12, 12-30 or 12, 12-14. 27
Lk. 4, 18-19

Catechism

430-440: Jesus, the Christ (the anointed one)

4th Sunday in Ordinary Time

Lectionary (72)

Jer. 1, 4-5. 17-19
Ps. 70 (71), 1-2. 3-4. 5-6. 15-17
1 Cor. 12, 31 - 13, 13 or 13, 4-13
Lk. 4, 21-30

Catechism

470-478: How the Son of God is a human person

5th Sunday in Ordinary Time

Lectionary (75)

Is. 6, 1-2. 3-8
Ps. 137 (138), 1-2. 2-3. 4-5. 7-8
1 Cor. 15, 1-11 or 15, 3-8. 11
Lk. 5, 1-11

Catechism

2794-2796: Our Father in heaven

6th Sunday in Ordinary Time

Lectionary (78)	Jer. 17, 5-8
	Ps. 1, 1-2. 3. 4. 6
	1 Cor. 15, 12. 16-20
	Lk. 6, 17. 20-26
Catechism	1716-1724: Our call to happiness

7th Sunday in Ordinary Time

Lectionary (81)	1 Sm. 26, 2. 7-9. 12-13. 22-23
	Ps. 102 (103), 1-2. 3-4. 8. 10. 12-13
	1 Cor. 15, 45-49
	Lk. 6, 27-38
Catechism	2544-2550: Poverty of heart; "I wish to see God"

8th Sunday in Ordinary Time

Lectionary (84)	Sir. 27, 4-7
	Ps. 91 (92), 2-3. 13-14. 15-16
	1 Cor. 15, 54-58
	Lk. 6, 39-45
Catechism	65-67: Jesus, mediator and fullness of all revelation

9th Sunday in Ordinary Time

Lectionary (87)	1 Kgs. 8, 41-43
	Ps. 116 (117), 1. 2
	Gal. 1, 1-2. 6-10
	Lk. 7, 1-10
Catechism	2142-2159: The Lord's name is holy (second commandment)

10th Sunday in Ordinary Time

Lectionary (90)	1 Kgs. 17, 17-24
	Ps. 29 (30), 2. 4. 5-6. 11. 12. 13
	Gal. 1, 11-19
	Lk. 7, 11-17
Catechism	1010-1014: The Christian meaning of death

11th Sunday in Ordinary Time

Lectionary (93)	2 Sm. 12, 7-10, 13
	Ps. 31 (32), 1-2. 5. 7. 11
	Gal 2, 16. 19-21
	Lk. 7, 36 - 8, 3 or 7, 36-50
Catechism	1987-1995: Justification

12th Sunday in Ordinary Time

Lectionary (96)	Zec. 12, 10-11
	Ps. 62 (63), 2. 3-4. 5-6. 8-9
	Gal. 3, 26-29
	Lk. 9, 18-24
Catechism	464-469: Jesus, truly God and truly human

13th Sunday in Ordinary Time

Lectionary (99)	1 Kgs. 19, 16. 19-21
	Ps. 15 (16), 1-2. 5. 7-8. 9-10. 11
	Gal. 5, 1. 13-18
	Lk. 9, 51-62
Catechism	144-149: The obedience of faith

14th Sunday in Ordinary Time

Lectionary (102)	Is. 66, 10-14
	Ps. 65 (66), 1-3. 4-5. 6-7. 16. 20
	Gal 6, 14-18
	Lk. 10, 1-12. 17-20 or 10, 1-9
Catechism	293-301: The world has been created for the glory of God; (Missionary activity "names" that God)

15th Sunday in Ordinary Time

Lectionary (105)	Dt. 30, 10-14
	Ps. 68 (69), 14. 17. 30-31. 33-34. 36. 37
	Col. 1, 15-20
	Lk. 10, 25-37
Catechism	1913-1916: Responsibility and participation

16th Sunday in Ordinary Time

Lectionary (108)	Gn. 18. 1-10
	Ps. 14 (15), 2-3. 3-4. 5
	Col. 1, 24-28
	Lk. 10, 38-42
Catechism	2725-2728: The struggle to pray

17th Sunday in Ordinary Time

Lectionary (111)	Gn. 18, 20-32
	Ps. 137 (138), 1-2. 2-3. 6-7. 7-8
	Col. 2, 12-14
	Lk. 11, 1-13
Catechism	2598-2619: The prayer of Jesus and Mary
	2734-2741: Child-like confidence in prayer

18th Sunday in Ordinary Time

Lectionary (114)	Eccl. 1, 2; 2, 21-23
	Ps. 94 (95), 1-2. 6-7. 8-9
	Col. 3, 1-5. 9-11
	Lk. 12, 13-21
Catechism	2534-2550: The tenth commandment
	1681-1683: Death as the Christian's final Pass-over
	988-1014: I believe in the resurrection of the body

19th Sunday in Ordinary Time

Lectionary (117)	Wis. 18, 6-9
	Ps. 32 (33), 1. 12. 18-19. 20-22
	Heb. 11, 1-2. 8-19 or 11, 1-2. 8-12
	Lk. 12, 32-48 or 12, 35-40
Catechism	27-35: Desire for God; approaches to the knowledge of God

20th Sunday in Ordinary Time

Lectionary (120)	Jer. 38, 4-6. 8-10
	Ps. 39 (40), 2. 3. 4. 18
	Heb. 12, 1-4
	Lk. 12, 49-53
Catechism	2302-2317: Safeguarding peace

21st Sunday in Ordinary Time

Lectionary (123)	Is. 66, 18-21
	Ps. 116 (117), 1. 2
	Heb. 12, 5-7. 11-13
	Lk. 13, 22-30
Catechism	1776-1785: Judgment of conscience; formation of conscience

22nd Sunday in Ordinary Time

Lectionary (126)	Sir. 3, 17-18. 20. 28-29
	Ps. 67 (68), 4-5. 6-7. 10-11
	Heb. 12, 18-19. 22-24
	Lk. 14, 1. 7-14
Catechism	2443-2449: Love for the poor

23rd Sunday in Ordinary Time

Lectionary (129)	Wis. 9, 13-18
	Ps. 89 (90), 3-4. 5-6. 12-13. 14-17
	Phlm. 9-10. 12-17
	Lk. 14. 25-33
Catechism	1720-1724: Christian happiness

24th Sunday in Ordinary Time

Lectionary (132)	Ex. 32, 7-11. 13-14
	Ps. 50 (51), 3-4. 12-13. 17. 19
	1 Tm. 1, 12-17
	Lk. 15, 1-32 or 15, 1-10
Catechism	2777-2785: We dare to approach in confidence to say: Our Father

25th Sunday in Ordinary Time

Lectionary (135)	Am. 8, 4-7
	Ps. 112 (113), 1-2. 4-6. 7-8
	1 Tm. 2, 1-8
	Lk. 16, 1-13 or 16, 10-13
Catechism	2407-2418: Respect for people and their goods
	2419-2436: The social doctrine of the church, economic activity, and social justice

26th Sunday in Ordinary Time

Lectionary (138)	Am. 6, 1. 4-7
	Ps. 145 (146), 7. 8-9. 9-10
	1 Tm. 6, 11-16
	Lk. 16, 19-31
Catechism	2437-2442: Justice and solidarity between nations

27th Sunday in Ordinary Time

Lectionary (141)	Hb. 1, 2-3; 2, 2-4
	Ps. 94 (95), 1-2. 6-7. 8-9
	2 Tm. 1, 6-8. 13-14
	Lk. 17, 5-10
Catechism	1996-2016: Grace and merit

28th Sunday in Ordinary Time

Lectionary (144)	2 Kgs. 5, 14-17
	Ps. 97 (98) 1, 2-3. 3-4
	2 Tm. 2, 8-13
	Lk. 17, 11-19
Catechism	2637-2643: Prayer of thanksgiving and praise

29th Sunday in Ordinary Time
Lectionary (147)   Ex. 17, 8-13
Ps. 120 (121), 1-2. 3-4. 5-6. 7-8
2 Tm. 3, 14 - 4, 2
Lk. 18, 1-8

Catechism   2629-2636: Prayer of petition and
intercession
2742-2745: Persevering in love

30th Sunday in Ordinary Time
Lectionary (150)   Sir. 35, 12-14. 16-18
Ps. 33 (34), 2-3. 17-18. 19. 23
2 Tm. 4, 6-8, 16-18
Lk. 18, 9-14

Catechism   2683-2691: Guidelines for prayer

31st Sunday in Ordinary Time
Lectionary (153)   Wis. 11, 22 - 12, 1
Ps. 144 (145), 1-2. 8-9. 10-11. 13. 14
2 Thes. 1, 11 - 2, 2
Lk. 19, 1-10

Catechism   976-983: I believe in the forgiveness of
sins

32nd Sunday in Ordinary Time
Lectionary (156)   2 Mc. 7, 1-2. 9-14
Ps. 16 (17), 1. 5-6. 8. 15
2 Thes. 2, 16 - 3, 5
Lk. 20, 27-38 or 20, 27. 34-38

Catechism   2566-2589: Prayer in Old and New
Testaments: the living God
1621-1654: Marriage and its qualities
(Marriage belongs to the present age
that is passing away)

33rd Sunday in Ordinary Time

Lectionary (159)

Mal. 3, 19-20
Ps. 97 (98), 5-6. 7-8. 9
2 Thes. 3, 7-12
Lk. 21, 5-19

Catechism

2729-2733: Humble watchfulness of heart

Last Sunday in Ordinary Time
Christ the King

Lectionary (163)

2 Sm. 5, 1-3
Ps. 121 (122), 1-2. 3-4. 4-5
Col. 1, 12-20
Lk. 23, 35-43

Catechism

2855-2856: For the kingdom the power and the glory are yours
1130: The sacraments of eternal life
671-674: Awaiting the subjection of all things in Jesus

Index to Catechism Paragraphs

Part I: The Profession of Faith

528:	Epiphany/ B
529:	Holy Family/ B
530:	Holy Family / A
533-537:	Baptism of the Lord / B
535-537:	Baptism of the Lord / C
538-540:	1 Lent/ A
541-546:	3 Lent/ C
554-556:	2 Lent/ A
577-582:	5 Lent/ C
583-586:	16 Year/ A
583-586:	3 Lent/ B
587-591:	Epiphany/ A
595-598:	4 Lent/ B
599-605:	24 Year/ B
599-605:	4 Lent/ B
606-618:	5 Lent/ B
641-644:	3 Easter/ C
645-646:	3 Easter/ B
651-655:	5 Lent/ A
651-655:	2 Easter/ B
659-664:	Ascension/ A
668-679:	Christ the King/ A
668-679:	Ascension/ C
671-674:	Christ the King/ C
702-716:	Pentecost/ B
717-720:	2 Advent/ C
721-726:	4 Advent/ C
727-730:	6 Easter/ A
731-732:	6 Easter/ C
731-741:	Pentecost/ A
737-741:	Ascension/ B
751-757:	11 Year/ B
759-769:	3 Advent/ B
771-801:	5 Easter/ B
797-798:	3 Lent/ B
830-856:	15 Year/ B
857-896:	4 Easter/ B
897-913:	13 Year/ A
914-933:	32 Year/ A
946-959:	33 Year A
964-970:	Motherhood of Mary/ C
976-983:	31 Year/ C
988-1014:	18 Year/ C
1010-1014:	10 Year/ C
1020-1022:	1 Advent/ A
1023-1029:	2 Lent/ A
1030-1032:	12 Year/ A

1033-1037:	12 Year/ A
1038-1041:	33 Year/ B
1042-1050:	4 Year/ B

Part II: Celebration of the Christian Mystery

1077-1083:	Trinity/ A
1077-1109:	Trinity/ C
1084-1109:	3 Easter/ A
1113-1130:	13 Year/ B
1122-1129:	13 Year/ B
1130:	Christ the King/ C
1217-1228:	Baptism of the Lord / A
1223-1225:	Baptism of the Lord / B
1226-1228:	Baptism of the Lord / B
1243-1244:	Trinity/ A
1262-1274:	4 Lent/ A
1262-1274:	3 Lent/ A
1285-1314:	6 Easter/ A
1324-1327:	20 Year/ B
1333-1336:	21 Year/ B
1333-1336:	Corpus Christi/ B
1373-1375:	3 Easter/ A
1373-1381:	Corpus Christi/ C
1382-1389:	Corpus Christi/ A
1382-1390:	17 Year/ B
1391-1401:	18 Year/ B
1396-1401:	5 Easter/ C
1402-1405:	19 Year/ B
1427-1449:	4 Lent/ C
1450-1460:	7 Year/ B
1499-1523:	5 Year/ B
1524-1525:	18 Year/ B
1539-1553:	4 Easter/ A
1554-1571:	11 Year/ A
1602-1617:	27 Year/ B
1618-1620:	32 Year/ A
1621-1654:	32 Year/ C
1643-1654:	27 Year/ B
1655-1658:	Holy Family/ C
1681-1683:	18 Year/ C

Part III: Life in Christ

1716-1724:	4 Year/ A
1716-1724:	6 Year/ C
1720-1742:	2 Advent/ A
1731-1738:	1 Advent/ B

1739-1742:	2 Advent/ A	2284-2301:	7 Year/ A
1739-1742:	2 Advent B	2302-2317:	20 Year/ C
1750-1756:	16 Year/ B	2331-2391:	5 Lent/ C
1762-1770:	12 Year/ B	2402-2406:	28 Year/ B
1776-1785:	21 Year/ C	2407-2418:	25 Year/ C
1776-1794:	22 Year/ B	2419-2436:	25 Year/ C
1814-1816:	4 Lent/ A	2437-2442:	26 Year/ C
1817-1821:	2 Lent/ C	2443-2449:	32 Year/ B
1822-1829:	30 Year/ A	2443-2449:	22 Year/ C
1822-1829:	31 Year/ B	2464-2474:	23 Year/ B
1822-1829:	5 Easter/ C	2471-2492:	Christ the King/ B
1830-1831:	Pentecost/ C	2493-2499:	5 Year/ A
1846-1848:	10 Year/ A	2500-2503:	5 Year/ A
1846-1869:	10 Year/ B	2514-2527:	6 Year/ A
1878-1885:	18 Year/ A	2534-2550:	18 Year/ C
1878-1889:	6 Easter/ B	2535-2543:	28 Year/ A
1886-1889:	23 Year/ A	2544-2500:	7 Year/ C
1897-1904:	6 Year/ B		
1905-1917:	29 Year/ B		

Part IV: Christian Prayer

1929-1938:	25 Year/ B	2566-2589:	32 Year/ C
1939-1942:	26 Year/ B	2598-2619:	17 Year/ C
1950-1964:	4 Advent/ A	2629-2636:	29 Year/ C
1965-1974:	3 Year/ A	2637-2643:	28 Year/ C
1987-1995:	11 Year/ C	2683-2691:	30 Year/ C
1987-2011:	15 Year/ A	2725-2728:	16 Year/ C
1996-2005:	25 Year/ A	2729-2733:	33 Year/ C
1996-2016:	27 Year/ C	2734-2741:	17 Year/ C
2006-2011:	26 Year/ A	2742-2745:	29 Year/ C
2012-2016:	9 Year/ A	2777-2785:	24 Year/ C
2030-2051:	16 Year/ B	2786-2793:	14 Year/ A
2044-2046:	6 Year/ A	2794-2796:	5 Year/ C
2084-2094:	22 Year/ A	2816-2821:	27 Year/ A
2084-2094:	8 Year/ B	2822-2827:	17 Year/ A
2095-2109:	31 Year/ A	2822-2827:	3 Advent/ C
2110-2159:	1 Lent/ B	2828-2837:	8 Year/ A
2142-2159:	9 Year/ C	2838-2845:	24 Year/ A
2168-2188:	9 Year/ B	2846-2854:	1 Advent/ C
2196-2233:	Holy Family/ A	2846-2854:	1 Lent/ C
2232-2233:	Holy Family/ C	2855-2856:	Christ the King/ C
2234-2246:	29 Year/ A		
2234-2243:	Holy Family/ C		
2259-2283:	5 Easter / A		